AN INFRASTRUCTURE GOVERNANCE APPROACH TO FISCAL MANAGEMENT IN STATE-OWNED ENTERPRISES AND PUBLIC–PRIVATE PARTNERSHIPS

NOVEMBER 2022

ASIAN DEVELOPMENT BANK

Contents

Table, Figures, and Box

Foreword

The Asia and Pacific region is committed to a climate-resilient and sustainable economic future even as it grapples with fiscal and debt pressures following the vast increase of public expenditure to drive economic recovery with the coronavirus disease (COVID-19) pandemic. The Russian invasion of Ukraine exacerbates these fiscal and debt concerns as sanctions on exports and supply chain disruptions from Black Sea ports severely impact the export of energy and food from Ukraine and the Russian Federation. The *Asian Development Outlook* of the Asian Development Bank (ADB) shows Brent crude oil spot prices increased 64.3% from June 2021 to June 2022.[1] The Food and Agriculture Organization of the United Nations (FAO) Food Price Index reached a historical high in February 2022, rising 21% over 2021.[2] The increase in wheat prices will affect countries where wheat is over 10% of the food consumer price index such as Armenia, India, Pakistan, the Philippines, the Republic of Korea, Sri Lanka, and Tajikistan. The rapid increase in energy and food prices will contribute to the growth of inflation in most ADB developing member countries (DMCs) of around 3.7% in 2022, compared to 2.5% in 2021.[3] Growth projections rebounded in 2021 from –0.8% to 6.9% for developing Asia, but remain below pre-pandemic growth rates in all subregions of Asia and the Pacific. The average fiscal deficit as a percent of gross domestic product (GDP) in emerging markets and middle-income countries in the Asia and Pacific region remained significant at –7.5% in 2020 and –6.29% in 2021, whereas low-income developing countries saw the fiscal deficit as a percentage of GDP grow from –2.27% in 2019 to –3.97% in 2021. Debt-to-GDP levels remain manageable overall, but the level of risk varies greatly among countries and regions. Sri Lanka stands out for debt that swelled from 78% of GDP in 2015 to just over 107% of GDP in 2021 and precipitated an economic crisis spurred by the pandemic.[4]

Considering the narrowing fiscal space, the increase in debt levels, the growing costs of disasters due to climate change, and an incomplete economic recovery, there is growing concern around the risk to government owners of state-owned enterprises (SOEs) and public–private partnerships (PPPs) that contingent liabilities—that is, liabilities that may occur depending on the outcome of an uncertain future event—and other fiscal risks may materialize with sizable costs to the budget. SOEs and PPPs deserve attention because there is already evidence that PPPs have characteristics that can obscure proper management and mitigation of fiscal costs and risks. PPPs are prone to the "fiscal illusion" arising from poor accountability for the management of contingent liabilities. SOE contingent liabilities and other fiscal risks, often undisclosed in public accounts, also pose a substantial fiscal risk if not properly accounted for and managed. This report describes infrastructure investment challenges in the Asia and

---

[1] ADB. 2022. *Asian Development Outlook (ADO) 2022 Supplement: Recovery Faces Diverse Challenges*. Manila.
[2] FAO Council, Hundred and Seventieth Session, 13–17 June 2022. Impact of the Ukraine–Russia conflict on global food security and related matters under the mandate of the FAO.
[3] ADB. 2022. *Asian Development Outlook (ADO) 2022: Mobilizing Taxes for Development*. Manila.
[4] Emerging markets and middle-income countries are defined according to the International Monetary Fund (IMF) classification according to factors such as market access, export diversification per capita income level, and the degree of integration into the global financial system. The low-income countries have per capital income levels below a threshold currently set at $2,700. For more information and full list of country groupings, see IMF. 2021. Methodological and Statistical Appendix I. *IMF Fiscal Monitor*.

Pacific region, provides evidence of the positive macroeconomic and fiscal effects of investing in quality infrastructure, and recommends a "gateway" assurance process at each stage of public investment management to improve investment quality and climate resilience, integration of upstream planning within the medium-term fiscal framework, and establishment of a standardized process for management of direct and contingent fiscal liabilities incurred by PPPs and SOEs.

Hiranya Mukhopadhyay
Chief of Governance Thematic Group
Sustainable Development and Climate Change Department
Asian Development Bank

Author Biographies

Hanif Rahemtulla, Principal Public Management Specialist

Hanif Rahemtulla is principal public management specialist at the Asian Development Bank. He is a public sector reform specialist focusing on public financial and investment management and fiscal decentralization with more than 20 years of experience in project management, advisory services, and research in more than 10 developing countries in the Asia and Pacific region. He obtained his doctoral degree from University College London and his postdoctoral degree from McGill University, Canada.

Michael Schur, Infrastructure Finance Specialist

Michael Schur has over 25 years of global experience as an infrastructure finance and investment specialist and has chief executive experience in both the public and private sectors. He is currently an independent board member of a private concessions investment company and advisor to private and public sector clients, both in Australia and internationally. He previously developed the commercial policy framework for state-owned enterprises in New South Wales, Australia, and the governance framework for public–private partnerships (PPPs) as inaugural head of the country's PPP unit in the National Treasury in South Africa.

David Bloomgarden, Public Investment Management Expert

David Bloomgarden is a public investment management expert with over 30 years of global experience in policy, management, and project design and implementation. As PPP and infrastructure governance consultant, he has advised the World Bank (Global Infrastructure Facility) and the Asian Development Bank on infrastructure governance and development of knowledge products on quality infrastructure investments. Prior to his current role, he was head of the upstream PPP unit of the Inter-American Development Bank, Multilateral Investment Fund, and served as chief of the Inclusive Cities Unit responsible for small and medium-sized enterprises lending and investments.

Acknowledgments

This report was led by Hanif Rahemtulla, principal public management specialist, Governance Thematic Group of ADB's Sustainable Development and Climate Change Department (SDTC-GOV); Michael Schur, infrastructure finance specialist; and David Bloomgarden, public investment management specialist. We acknowledge the helpful comments provided by Hiranya Mukhopadhyay, chief, SDTC-GOV; Adrian Torres, Chief of PPP-TGS, OPPP; Joao Pedro Farinha, principal financial sector economist, Public Management, Financial Sector, and Trade Division, Central and West Asia Department; David Aaron Robinett, senior public management specialist (state-owned enterprise reforms), SDTC-GOV; Agustina Musa, senior financial management specialist, Southeast Asia Department; and Stella Balgos, consultant, SDTC-GOV.

Abbreviations

ADB	Asian Development Bank
COVID-19	coronavirus disease
DMC	developing member country
GDP	gross domestic product
GIH	Global Infrastructure Hub
IMF	International Monetary Fund
IPSAS	International Public Sector Accounting Standard
MoF	Ministry of Finance
OECD	Organisation for Economic Co-operation and Development
PFRAM	Public–Private Partnership Fiscal Risk Assessment Model
PIE-X	Public Investment Efficiency Index
PIM	public investment management
PIMA	Public Investment Management Assessment
PPA	power purchase agreement
PPP	public–private partnership
QII	quality infrastructure investment
SOE	state-owned enterprise
VFM	value for money

1. Introduction

The trilemma of substantial infrastructure gaps, lower revenue, and higher debt levels, following the coronavirus disease (COVID-19) economic contraction compounded by the impacts of climate change, represent the perfect storm constraining public infrastructure investment in Asia. The need for short-term fiscal stimulus to manage the impact of COVID-19 created financial risks for many countries leading to a period of fiscal consolidation. Central government expenditure rose by an average of 3.06% of gross domestic product (GDP) from 2019 to 2020. The largest increase was in South Asia, which recorded the largest expenditure increase of 4.93% of GDP, followed by East Asia with an increase of 3.55% of GDP, and Southeast Asia with an increase of 2.27%. The Pacific region had the lowest expenditure increase of 1.3% between 2020 and 2021, albeit starting from a high level of government expenditure as a share of GDP.[5] Fiscal risks have also been exacerbated by the Russian invasion of Ukraine and higher interest rates, COVID-19 variants, inflation, and supply chain disruptions. The external debt of regional members of the Asian Development Bank (ADB) will increase by 9% of GDP between 2020 and 2022. Around 20% of developing member countries (DMCs)—Bhutan, Fiji, India, the Lao People's Democratic Republic, Maldives, Mongolia, Pakistan, and Sri Lanka—are above the "high scrutiny threshold" of the International Monetary Fund (IMF) for monitoring public debt.[6] Reducing public infrastructure investment and redirecting the available fiscal space toward short-term stimulus was a rational policy response during the height of COVID-19. However, there is a downside: the loss of medium- and long-term benefits of quality infrastructure investment to improve access to infrastructure service and help meet critical Sustainable Development Goals such as access to clear water and sanitation, affordable and clean energy, sustainable cities, and climate action.[7]

ADB's *Asian Development Outlook* (2022) shows economic recovery of 5.2% in 2022 and 5.3% in 2023, which should help to reduce vulnerability to external shocks in most countries. A key challenge for economic recovery will be to mobilize sufficient tax revenue as a percentage of GDP combined with more efficient public investment to create employment, stimulate economic growth, address climate change, and enhance the quality of life. Public investment will need to be a vital component of the post-COVID-19 recovery in the context of higher debt, fiscal consolidation, and the need to invest in climate resilience and mitigation. This is because there is compelling evidence that efficient and productive infrastructure investment will not only raise GDP, but will cause debt-to-GDP ratios to fall and maximize the economic and fiscal gains in a fiscally constrained environment. For decision-makers to ensure fiscal sustainability, facilitate GDP growth, and lower debt-to-GDP levels, it is critically important that such investment is of the highest possible quality—that is, the right infrastructure delivering maximum economic benefits at the lowest cost. This will require investment of a different kind—investment in sound institutions, governance frameworks, and integration of climate costs and benefits in public financial management to deliver high-quality, green, inclusive, and resilient infrastructure.

---

[5] ADB. 2022. *Asian Development Outlook*. Manila.
[6] B. Ferrarini, M. Giugale, and J. Pradelli, eds. 2022. *The Sustainability of Asia's Debt, Problems, Policies, and Practices.* Manila: ADB.
[7] ADB. 2021. *Supporting Quality Infrastructure in Developing Asia*. Manila.

Contingent liabilities are sizable in many countries and, thus, pose a risk to public finance especially for public–private partnerships (PPPs) and state-owned enterprises (SOEs) which merit extra attention by public finance authorities. Unlike conventional public investments, PPPs can escape fiscal scrutiny. As long-term contracts, PPPs may transfer a significant volume of risks to private operators, paying the corresponding risk premium, or they can pay a lower direct cost, hiding fiscal risks in the PPP contract. Similarly, SOEs typically have complex fiscal arrangements with governments. Much of government support for SOEs is direct, in the form of subsidies, current transfers, and capital injections, but government support is also in the form of on-lending, loans, and lending guarantees. These arrangements have the potential to create fiscal risks if not appropriately managed and fully disclosed in the budget and financial statements. Poor oversight of SOE investments by governments can exacerbate these risks. According to the World Bank, data on liabilities of low-income developing countries report contingent liabilities from PPPs in less than 10% of the cases, and official government statistic often report on direct debt only, omitting SOE debt.[8] In East Asia and the Pacific, only 12% of countries record explicit and contingent liabilities arising from PPPs in the national accounts as compared to 87% in high-income Organisation for Economic Co-operation and Development (OECD) countries.[9] Fiscal governance reforms will vary by country depending on institutional capacity. Reforms should aim to integrate PPPs with infrastructure planning and the medium-term fiscal framework, and incorporate processes for effective contingent liability management, including a strong, standardized project approval process with coordination and final approval by a central agency such as the Ministry of Finance or Treasury.

---

[8]   World Bank. 2021. *Debt Transparency in Developing Economies*. Washington, DC. The term "LIDC" refers generally to the World Bank's International Development Association borrowers which corresponds to Asian Development Fund (ADF)-borrowing countries. For the current 2022 fiscal year, the World Bank defines low-income economies as countries whose gross national income (GNI) per capita is $1,045 or less in 2020; for lower-middle-income economies, the GNI per capita is between $1,046 and $4,095; for upper-middle-income economies, between $4,096 and $12,695; and for high-income economies, equal to or greater than $12,696.

[9]   World Bank. 2020. *Benchmarking Infrastructure Development 2020: Assessing Regulatory Quality to Prepare, Procure, and Manage PPPs and Traditional Public Investment in Infrastructure Projects*. Washington, DC. The countries included for Asia and OECD by the World Bank can be found at Benchmarking Infrastructure-development-2020.

2. Asia Infrastructure Investment Challenges

The Asia and Pacific region is forecast to require $26.2 trillion, or $1.7 trillion per year, to restore its growth momentum, eliminate poverty, and address climate change.** Most of this investment is in economic and social infrastructure, including $434 billion annually for clean energy, climate resilience, and adaptation, and as much as $196 billion annually for transport, water supply and sanitation, and other public infrastructure (Figure 1).

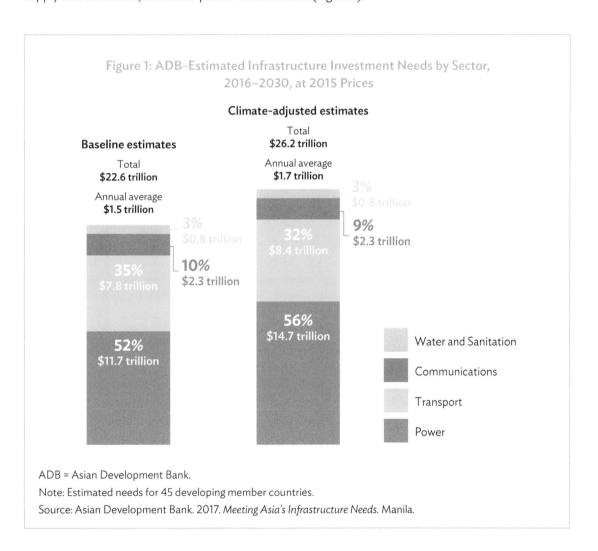

Figure 1: ADB-Estimated Infrastructure Investment Needs by Sector, 2016–2030, at 2015 Prices

Climate-adjusted estimates

Baseline estimates

Baseline estimates
Total
$22.6 trillion
Annual average
$1.5 trillion

3%
$0.8 trillion
35%
$7.8 trillion
10%
$2.3 trillion
52%
$11.7 trillion

Climate-adjusted estimates
Total
$26.2 trillion
Annual average
$1.7 trillion

3%
$0.8 trillion
32%
$8.4 trillion
9%
$2.3 trillion
56%
$14.7 trillion

Water and Sanitation

Communications

Transport

Power

ADB = Asian Development Bank.
Note: Estimated needs for 45 developing member countries.
Source: Asian Development Bank. 2017. *Meeting Asia's Infrastructure Needs.* Manila.

3

While increased infrastructure spending will help accelerate economic recovery in some countries, other countries may not have the fiscal capacity to increase spending due to their revenue and debt levels. The worsening of the debt situation and extremely limited fiscal space and inflationary trends can lead to higher interest costs and reduced infrastructure investments, and the need to prioritize spending on the most urgent projects. It is critical to balance the vital demand for infrastructure financing with an emphasis on increasing investment efficiency and integrating and strengthening the policy, legal, regulatory, and institutional frameworks in traditional public sector investments, SOEs, and PPPs (footnote 7).

DMCs with strong public investment management (PIM) institutions have more credible, predictable, and efficient investments that deliver economic, social, and environmental objectives with better development impact.[10] Stronger infrastructure governance is associated with the improvement of both the quality and volume of infrastructure investment and implementation. Improved PIM and better integration of the development and current budgets will ensure projects are built on time and within budget, thereby containing risks of ensuing debt buildup. An essential driver of infrastructure governance is investment efficiency. The IMF finds that countries in Asia and the Pacific lose 32% on average of the potential economic benefits of public investment due to inefficiencies in the investment process, and lower-income economies have a greater efficiency gap of up to 40%.[11] This pricing of efficiency loss leads to projects that are not correctly costed during upstream project preparation to account for risks, including climate risks, nor are those costs incorporated in the medium-term expenditure framework as an input into public investment decisions. The spider diagram in Figure 2 is the IMF Public Investment Management Assessment (PIMA) for Asia and the Pacific. PIMA evaluates institutional design which considers factors such as the organizational rules and procedures on paper and institutional effectiveness to assess the degree to which the intended purpose of the institution is achieved and has impact. The results show that countries tend to score higher on institutional design then on effectiveness, particularly for project selection, project appraisal, and project implementation.

Improvements in service delivery are closely associated with strengthening SOE governance and the role of SOEs in infrastructure development, including for PPPs that SOEs design and implement. Weak SOE governance and oversight, underfunded policy mandate, and weak institutional capacity at the enterprise level to manage risks and resources can negatively affect public finances resulting from lower profitability and financial losses. These factors result in substantial fiscal transfers from the national government budget, and the creation of high SOE indebtedness and other contingent liabilities. Poor SOE governance can also increase the costs of constructing and operating infrastructure and lower its quality, and may weaken potential opportunities to attract other sources of finance. It is also a source of allocative inefficiency in the economy. SOE reforms can help to reduce these liabilities by professionalizing the management of SOE assets and liabilities on the balance sheet of SOEs, and allowing for scalability through nonsovereign borrowing by SOEs. These types of reforms create sovereign fiscal space, improve access to finance for infrastructure investment, and improve SOE management.

---

[10] PIM institutions refer to public sector institutions that are involved in the planning, allocation, and implementing of public investments. It is a subset of budget institutions that oversee the public financial management process.
[11] IMF. 2018. *Public Investment Management Review and Update*. Washington, DC. To measure country infrastructure governance capability, the IMF developed the Public Investment Framework to evaluate infrastructure governance based on an analysis of institutions that cover the three stages of the public investment cycle: planning, allocation, and implementation. It assesses institutions from three perspectives: institutional design and roles, effectiveness, and reform priorities.

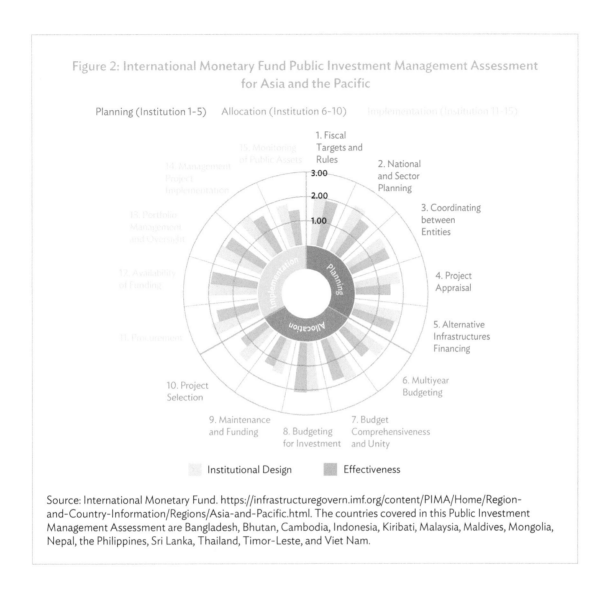

Figure 2: International Monetary Fund Public Investment Management Assessment for Asia and the Pacific

Source: International Monetary Fund. https://infrastructuregovern.imf.org/content/PIMA/Home/Region-and-Country-Information/Regions/Asia-and-Pacific.html. The countries covered in this Public Investment Management Assessment are Bangladesh, Bhutan, Cambodia, Indonesia, Kiribati, Malaysia, Maldives, Mongolia, Nepal, the Philippines, Sri Lanka, Thailand, Timor-Leste, and Viet Nam.

Private sector participation in the development and operation of public service assets is needed to provide additional resources to supplement traditional public investment. Sound governance practices for PPP programs and projects should be adapted and implemented especially in developing countries lacking well-developed national infrastructure governance institutions. Government decision-makers should not view the use of PPP procurement as a panacea to solve fiscal constraints. International experience with PPPs has led to the concept of a "fiscal illusion" that places PPPs off-budget and not accounted for as contingent liabilities and public debt. Countries also need to ensure that the investment decision is first based on value for money (VFM) and cost–benefit analysis to determine if a project optimizes efficiency and effectiveness through the allocation of risks between the public and private sectors. Once the project analysis shows that a project achieves greater VFM relative to other potential projects in the pipeline, the next step is for government to decide on the best procurement option—traditional infrastructure procurement or PPP.[12]

---

[12]   ADB. 2022. *An Infrastructure Governance Approach to PPP Value for Money Analysis.* Manila.

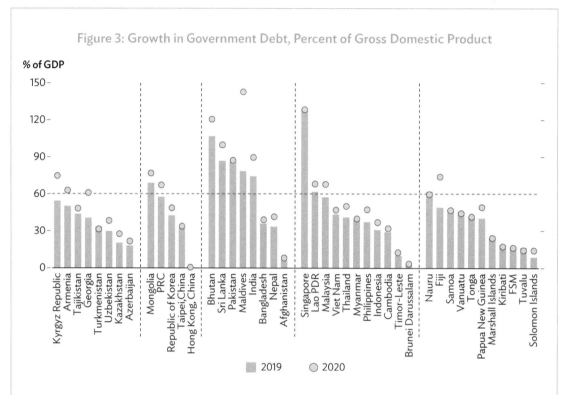

Figure 3: Growth in Government Debt, Percent of Gross Domestic Product

FSM = Federated States of Micronesia, GDP = gross domestic product, Lao PDR = Lao People's Democratic Republic, PRC = People's Republic of China.

Notes:
1. The Pacific excludes the Cook Islands, Niue, and Palau, as no data available for these economies.
2. ADB placed on hold its assistance in Afghanistan effective 15 August 2021. This report was prepared based on information available for Afghanistan as of 31 July 2021. The information/data on Afghanistan was collected from international sources.

Source: International Monetary Fund. 2021. World Economic Outlook April 2021 Database. https://www.imf.org/en/Publications/WEO/weo-database/2021/April.

The last 10 years has seen the most rapid increase in global debt in the past 50 years. Since 2010, developing country debt rose by 60 percentage points of GDP to a historic peak of more than 170% of GDP in 2019. Even excluding the People's Republic of China, debt grew by 20 percentage points of GDP, reaching 108%.[13] As expected, COVID-19 impacted public debt levels and fiscal balances. In Asia and the Pacific, as shown in Figure 3, gross public debt rose in 2020, but remained below 60% of GDP in most economies. COVID-19 continues to impact government tax revenues and extraordinary levels of government expenditure in the form of income support and health-related responses.

As the highly accommodative fiscal stance of governments gives way to fiscal consolidation and interest rates rise, this could engender higher borrowing costs in the medium term for cash-strapped governments with already elevated levels of debt. The Debt Sustainability Analysis introduced by the IMF categorizes 16 ADB DMCs as ranging from low to high debt-distressed countries as can be seen in Figure 4.

---

[13]   M. A. Kose et al. 2020. Caught by a Cresting Debt Wave. *Finance & Development*, Vol. 57.

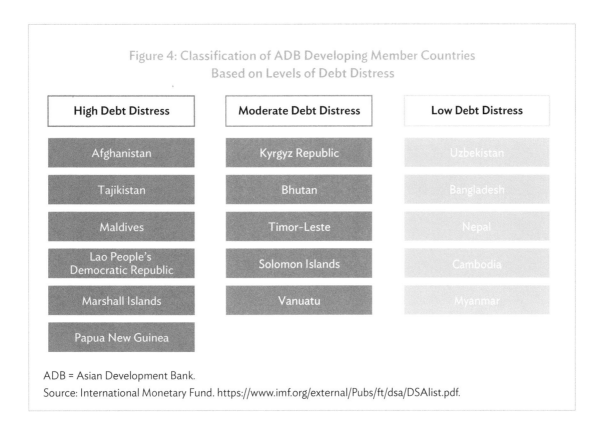

Figure 4: Classification of ADB Developing Member Countries
Based on Levels of Debt Distress

High Debt Distress	Moderate Debt Distress	Low Debt Distress
Afghanistan	Kyrgyz Republic	Uzbekistan
Tajikistan	Bhutan	Bangladesh
Maldives	Timor-Leste	Nepal
Lao People's Democratic Republic	Solomon Islands	Cambodia
Marshall Islands	Vanuatu	Myanmar
Papua New Guinea		

ADB = Asian Development Bank.
Source: International Monetary Fund. https://www.imf.org/external/Pubs/ft/dsa/DSAlist.pdf.

Addressing the substantial infrastructure challenges identified above may require taking unprecedented debt levels even higher. However, borrowing can be beneficial for all economies, and especially developing countries, if government debt is used to finance investment with high GDP growth potential, such as public infrastructure as well as education and health care, that generate strong social and economic returns.[14] At the same time, whereas fiscal policy was accommodative in response to the COVID-19 pandemic, this will tighten quite considerably in many regional economies in 2022 and beyond. In Figure 5, the definition of fiscal impulse refers to the variation in the fiscal balance, expressed as a percentage of GDP, from the prior year. The diamonds denote the change in fiscal balance compared to the 5-year average (2015–2019). Positive changes in the fiscal balance show fiscal consolidation; negative changes show fiscal expansion. In 2022, the data show the most fiscal consolidation in Hong Kong, China; Singapore; Mongolia; Brunei Darussalam; the Philippines; and Sri Lanka. In almost all the countries, these listed below the level of fiscal consolidation in 2023 and will remain well above the pre-pandemic levels of 2015–2019.

---

[14]   S. Gupta et al. 2014. Efficiency-Adjusted Public Capital and Growth. *World Development 57.* (C): pp. 164–178; IMF. 2015. *Making Public Investment More Efficient.* Washington, DC.

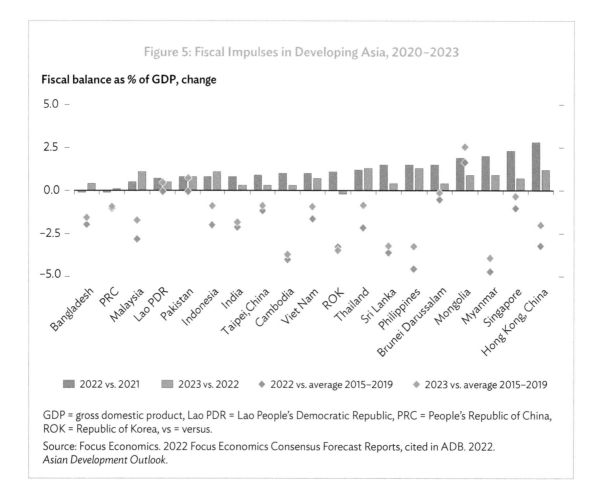

Figure 5: Fiscal Impulses in Developing Asia, 2020–2023

GDP = gross domestic product, Lao PDR = Lao People's Democratic Republic, PRC = People's Republic of China, ROK = Republic of Korea, vs = versus.

Source: Focus Economics. 2022 Focus Economics Consensus Forecast Reports, cited in ADB. 2022. *Asian Development Outlook*.

3. Investing in Quality Infrastructure

ADB and other development banks can provide support through infrastructure governance diagnostics, knowledge products, and technical guidance to help DMCs implement quality infrastructure investment (QII). QII aims to improve the overall efficiency of public and private infrastructure.[15] Investment in infrastructure should have positive effects on growth and the fiscal position; the economic benefits will exceed the economic costs provided the investment is economically efficient. All governments invest in infrastructure projects that they believe to be beneficial. These benefits can flow as direct fiscal impacts—where the project revenues exceed the costs—or as indirect fiscal impact— where the resulting GDP growth flows through in increased taxation. While there are short-term stimulus effects from all infrastructure investment, in the long term, the macroeconomic impact through increased economic growth is largely dependent on the quality and economic efficiency of the investment.

An increase in public investment raises both short- and long-term output and is essential to grapple with limited fiscal space from the trilemma of substantial infrastructure gaps, high debt levels, and the COVID-19-induced economic contraction. In an analysis of 17 OECD countries, the IMF similarly found that an increase of 1% of GDP in public investment increases output by approximately 0.4% in 1 year after the investment, and by about 1.5% 4 years after the investment, resulting in a fiscal multiplier of about 1.4.[16] The study also found that public investment shocks significantly affect output, but the effects were found to be significantly more robust in countries with greater public investment efficiency, almost four times as much, both in the short and medium term. Under conditions of slack in the economy and monetary accommodation, the increase in output from more public investment may surpass the issuance of debt to finance the investment. This result is not guaranteed, however; increasing investment quality (i.e., efficiency and productivity) is essential to mitigate the trade-off between higher economic output and higher public-debt-to-GDP ratios. Other studies corroborate these findings. The World Bank, for example, in a review of fiscal adjustments undertaken by several countries in the 1990s, found that investment in high-efficiency infrastructure can result in a reduction in the public debt-to-GDP ratio. More recently, the Global Infrastructure Hub (GIH), in a large study of fiscal multipliers, found that public investment, the fiscal spending category which includes infrastructure investment, has a cumulative impact on GDP of at least 1.5 after 2 to 5 years.[17] These studies confirm that the positive relationship between levels of

---

[15] The G20 Finance Ministers' and Central Bank Governors' Meeting in Fukuoka, Japan (8–9 June 2019) endorsed QII calling for "maximizing the positive impact of infrastructure to achieve sustainable growth and development while preserving the sustainability of public finances, raising economic efficiency in view of life-cycle cost, integrating environmental and social considerations, including women's economic empowerment, building resilience against natural hazards and other risks, and strengthening infrastructure governance." Available at https://www.mof.go.jp/english/international_policy/convention/g20/annex6_1.pdf.

[16] IMF. 2015. *The Macroeconomic Effects of Public Investment: Evidence from Advanced Economies (Working paper)*.

[17] The GIH preliminary findings on quantifying the economic impact of infrastructure investment Third G20 Infrastructure Working Group: Virtual Meeting 9 June 2020 Preliminary Findings. The GIH analyzed over 3,000 estimates of the fiscal multiplier—a ratio of the increase in GDP after 1 year (impact multiplier) and at 2–5 years (cumulative multiplier) that results from an increase in public spending—from over 200 academic papers from the last 25 years. GIH also analyzed over 600 estimates of the effect of public investment on long-run productivity, from 170 academic papers.

GDP and gross fixed capital formation, and that the economic impact of public investment is higher than all other forms of public spending, especially in the medium term.

An objective measure of quality infrastructure enables decision makers to quantify the benefits of investing in infrastructure and to measure efficiencies of individual countries to highlight specific areas for improvement. The IMF has developed the Public Investment Efficiency Index (PIE-X) as a comprehensive measure and applied it to over 100 countries.[18] PIE-X assesses the relationship between the capital stock of public sector infrastructure compared to indicators that measure access to infrastructure services and the quality of infrastructure assets. Countries that have the highest scores for their levels of infrastructure coverage and quality (output) for a given level of public capital stock and income per capita (inputs) represent an efficiency frontier as shown in Figure 6.

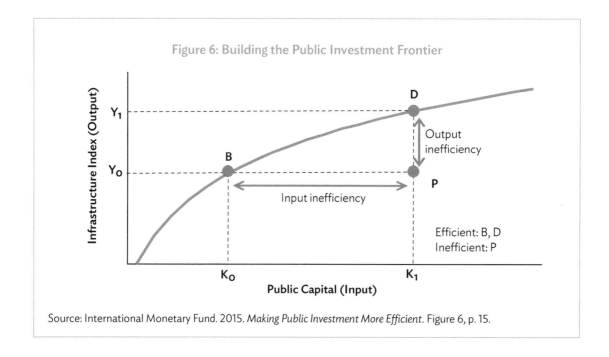

Figure 6: Building the Public Investment Frontier

Source: International Monetary Fund. 2015. *Making Public Investment More Efficient.* Figure 6, p. 15.

The IMF assessment assigns a PIE-X score of between 0 and 1, determined by the vertical distance to the frontier relative to best performers. Countries that have a longer distance from the frontier are less efficient in their public investment and have a lower PIE-X score.[19] PIE-X estimates confirm that there is considerable opportunity to improve public investment efficiency in most countries. The average efficiency gap for the Asia and Pacific region is 32%, as shown in Figure 7.

---

[18]   IMF. 2015. *Making Public Investment More Efficient.*
[19]   Country PIE-X scores derive from three data sets:
   • a physical indicator combining data on the volume of infrastructure such as electricity production, access to water, miles of paved roads, and others;
   • an indicator using the World Economic Forum's survey of business leader's impressions of the quality of key infrastructure services; and
   • a hybrid indicator combining the physical and survey-based indicators into a synthetic index of the quality and coverage of infrastructure assets.

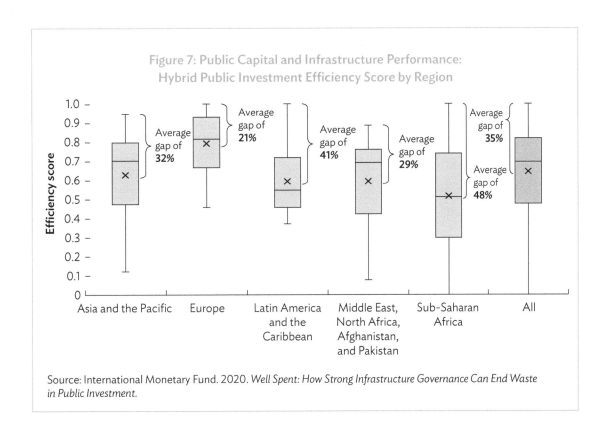

Figure 7: Public Capital and Infrastructure Performance:
Hybrid Public Investment Efficiency Score by Region

Source: International Monetary Fund. 2020. *Well Spent: How Strong Infrastructure Governance Can End Waste in Public Investment.*

There is a range of GDP outcomes from higher-quality infrastructure spending based on factors such as the annual spend, the level of efficiency, and the fiscal multiplier. A hypothetical quantification can be provided of the potential benefits of higher-quality infrastructure where quality is defined as infrastructure that is well planned, well implemented, resilient, and sustainable. The dual effects of public investment on economic growth—through efficiency (i.e., the amount of physical infrastructure for a given investment spend) and productivity (i.e., the multiplier effect of the investment on economic growth)—is summarized in the table. This hypothetical analysis assesses the range of potential efficiency and productivity impacts of differing reductions in the average 32% public investment efficiency gap for the region, based on the forecast $1.5 trillion annual investment requirement (4% of regional GDP), from 2016 to achieve the Sustainable Development Goals by 2030. The table shows that as the region moves up the PIE-X frontier by increasing investment efficiency, thereby reducing the average 32 % public investment efficiency gap, there are dual impacts, on efficiency and productivity. While it is not conceivable that the entire efficiency gap can be eliminated, the table provides an indication of the potentially significant growth benefits of investing in quality infrastructure.

Infrastructure Investment—Estimates of Annual Benefits from Efficiency and Productivity Associated with Quality Infrastructure

% Reduction in Efficiency Gap	Annual Spend (trillion)	% GDP	Efficiency Gain (% GDP)	Productivity Gain (% GDP)[a]	Impact on GDP Growth[b]
Base Case	1.5	4.0	--	--	--
Eff 1 (8% gain)	1.4	3.7	0.3	0.5	8.9%
Eff 2 (16% gain)	1.3	3.4	0.6	0.9	16.4%
Eff 3 (32 % gain)	1.1	2.9	1.1	1.6	30.3%

Eff = efficiency, GDP = gross domestic product.

[a] Based on fiscal multiplier of 1.5.

[b] Based on 2022 regional growth forecast of 5.4%.

Source: Authors' own data analysis. The data is based on Public Investment Management Assessment (PIMA) findings on public investment management (PIM) efficiency. The International Monetary Fund (IMF) uses the data envelopment analysis methodology, a common model in the literature based on nonparametric methods to calculate public investment efficiency. Findings are estimations because data on capital stock and investment spending are not always available or reliable across countries and among line ministries, state-owned enterprises (SOEs), and public–private partnerships (PPPs). For a full description of assumption in PIMA methodology, see https://www.imf.org/external/np/pp/eng/2015/061115.pdf. With these assumptions in mind, the calculation works as follows: it calculates the impact on efficiency and productivity were the region able to reduce the average public investment efficiency gap relative to the IMF's Public Investment Efficiency Index (PIE-X) frontier. It assumes an average fiscal multiplier of 1.5, while acknowledging variations around this average. The efficiency calculations, measured in % GDP terms, compare the annual spend on infrastructure against a base case 4.0%, for varying levels of increased efficiency. The productivity calculations assess the productivity gain derived from the fiscal multiplier effect of more efficient investment, and then calculate the impact of this on forecast growth of 5.4 % for 2022 (e.g., growth would be 8.9 % higher—i.e., 5.9 % rather than 5.4 %—if public investment was 8% more efficient). It also shows that a reduction of the efficiency gap would reduce the required level of public investment from 1.5 trillion to 1.1 trillion if efficiency gains are 32%, while generating over 30% increase in regional growth.

4. Sources of Efficiency Gaps in Infrastructure Investment

In many countries, a major proportion of public infrastructure investment is delivered by the central government through various government agencies and ministries. This is very typical for infrastructure such as health, transport, and education. For most governments, this is the default option—public infrastructure is delivered directly. A defining feature of this delivery model is that the ministries and agencies are budget-dependent, that is, their expenditures—both operating and capital—are made from the government budget and the revenue from the provision of services flows into the government budget. Government annual budgeting processes are generally rigorous with either explicit or implicit limitations on budget deficits and debt raising. The annual budget process typically seeks to ensures a high degree of transparency and oversight: expenditure allocations are scrutinized, and actual results reported. Revenues from charges by the government departments or agencies are also budgeted (essentially forecast) and actual revenues reported. In the short term, investment is explicitly constrained by fiscal limits.

In response to many of the inadequacies of traditional infrastructure delivery, several governments have turned to alternative financing and delivery modalities such as PPPs and SOEs. A major cause of inefficiency in infrastructure delivery is that the fiscal costs and risks of a project are given inadequate consideration in the project development process, typically due to suboptimal project governance. SOEs and PPPs promise greater efficiency in infrastructure delivery and have the potential to reduce the efficiency gap—if designed and governed appropriately. In the case of SOEs, through a stronger commercial focus and potentially greater autonomy; and in the case of PPPs, through harnessing private sector initiatives for performance. Both modalities can realize efficiency improvements. However, they also have the potential to expose governments to considerable direct and contingent liabilities, if the policy settings that govern their operations are not properly developed.

This government budgetary process does not always ensure that public infrastructure investment is efficient and successful. Investment is more than just construction: it is the complete life cycle, from project conception, selection, justification, through design, planning, construction, completion, and then maintenance and operation of the finished facility. At all stages of the process, there are possibilities of failure, resulting in cost overruns and delays, failure to deliver an appropriate service, and/or failure to realize benefits and unintended consequences. In theory, all projects that are economically viable can be financed—that is, there are no fiscal limits due to positive economic and financial returns of efficient infrastructure investment. In practice, since all infrastructure investments involve some risks, there are always financial constraints—financiers and, indeed, governments will always want a buffer as not all projects will turn out exactly as planned.

There is a high degree of "optimism bias" in the projected capital costs of projects contributing to the efficiency gap and giving rise to fiscal risks and costs. This occurs partly because the budget process is to a degree competitive and partly from the enthusiasm of agencies to get their projects off the ground. This starts at the project development and selection stage and continues through the entire life cycle. Once finance has been allocated and construction begins, it is difficult to terminate a project that runs over time and budget. While investment in the capital cost of an infrastructure project may be approved, the expenditure required to operate and maintain the facility is subject to the discretion of the legislature on an annual basis. The *World Bank PPP Reference Guide Version 3* cites multiple studies showing the most common causes of optimism bias are the overestimation of benefits leading to larger, more complex projects than are justified by the demand for services and the underestimation of costs.[20] More subtle and harder to quantify are projects that were funded ahead of more worthy candidates or projects that did not deliver the promised benefits or achieve the expected value for money.[21]

In many Asian economies, SOEs are significant players in the infrastructure market for both PPP and traditional infrastructure procurement methodologies. They provide essential public services, such as transport; utilities (electricity, water, and gas); and exploration of natural resources (oil, gas, mining). They build and operate key public infrastructure—for example, around 55% of electricity generating capacity in the Asia and Pacific region is owned and operated by SOEs. SOEs, on average, represent a bigger share of GDP in developing countries than in advanced countries. SOE investments represented 74% of total infrastructure investment in East Asia and the Pacific, of which 84% is from the People's Republic of China (60%) and Indonesia (24%). In South Asia, SOEs accounted for 44% of total infrastructure investment.[22]

There are many sound reasons for governments to establish and reform SOEs and deliver infrastructure services through SOEs. Most importantly, to the extent they can borrow from commercial lenders on commercial terms, independent of government support, they can provide governments with additional fiscal headroom to finance other pressing priorities, as well as create larger incentives for productivity. The desire to create fiscal space on government balance sheets is often a primary reason why governments establish SOEs in the first place.[23] And there has been some success in this regard. Following two decades of reliance on government direct transfers, by end-2015, commercial SOE debt in emerging markets amounted to around $1.4 trillion. State-owned banks and financial institutions are a large part of the Asia and Pacific financial systems, accounting for 40% or more of banking system assets in a number of countries. Financial and nonfinancial SOEs globally are among the largest firms and are major issuers of securities.[24] Nonfinancial cooperate debt varies, but is as high as 86% in the People's Republic of China, 80% in Malaysia, 65% in India, and 22% in Indonesia.[25]

---

[20]   World Bank. 2017. *PPP Reference Guide Version 3*. Washington, DC. p. 24.
[21]   World Bank. 2017. *Governance Approach to Value for Money*.
[22]   World Bank, PPIAF. 2019. Who Sponsors Infrastructure Projects? Disentangling Public and Private Contributions. Cited in ADB. 2021. *Supporting Quality Infrastructure in Developing Member Countries of the Asian Development Bank*. Manila.
[23]   ADB. 2021. *The Bankable SOE: Commercial Financing for State-Owned Enterprises*. Manila.
[24]   ADB. 2020. *Guidance Note on State-Owned Enterprises Reform in Sovereign Projects and Programs*. Manila.
[25]   M. Jamrisko, A. Nag, and K. Salna. 2020. Emerging-Market Debt Crisis Brews as State Firms Need Rescue. *Bloomberg*. 11 June. https://www.bloomberg.com/news/articles/2020-06-11/rescuing-state-owned-firms-adds-to-emerging-market-debt-crisis. Cited in ADB. 2021. *The Bankable SOE: Commercial Financing for State-Owned Enterprises*. Manila, Philippines.

While there are many positive aspects of SOEs, they are a potential source of inefficiency and create fiscal risks for government. The main source arises through the governance structures of SOEs and their financial relationship with governments. There are conflicting objectives; SOEs must be commercially viable and provide services at below cost while maintaining employment. From a financial viewpoint, SOEs likely have a degree of independence from government as well as having access to finance from the government on "favorable" terms.

SOE reform in sovereign projects and programs is not easy nor quick, and faces multiple implementation challenges. These challenges include diffused and weak accountability; multiple mandates, subsidies, political influence, and preferred treatment relative to private sector competitors; and poor governance especially as it relates to the disclosure of assets and liabilities.[26] Separately, and noting similar disclosure issues around SOEs globally, the World Bank recently estimated that the average SOE debt levels (domestic and external) are 7.3% of GDP and are broadly distributed across countries (ranging from 0.4% to 18.1%).[27]

Governments and SOEs typically have complex fiscal arrangements. Much of this support is direct, in the form of subsidies, current transfers, and capital injections, but as much of it is contingent, in the form of on-lending, loans, and lending guarantees (Figure 8). These arrangements have the potential to create fiscal risks if not appropriately managed and fully disclosed in the budget and financial statements. **The single most important fiscal risk arising from SOEs' poor performance is the creation of contingent liabilities arising from government guarantees of SOE debt obligations.** In their dealings with the private sector, there is a tendency for parties to require governments to explicitly guarantee the obligations of SOEs. This may take the form of debt guarantees to lenders or guarantees for payment under long-term contracts such as power purchase agreements. Debt guarantees would likely enable the SOE to borrow at a lower cost—the government's cost of debt, effectively using the government's more favorable credit rating. An alternative form of guarantee is for the government to borrow and on-lend to the SOE. At the same time, many Asian governments issue guarantees to SOEs to facilitate private capital market financing of infrastructure investments, with the understanding that it allows them to borrow from private capital markets based on the government's credit rating, thus lowering, or appearing to lower, the cost of capital for infrastructure borrowing.

Even where formal guarantees are not in place, moral hazard issues facing SOE financing arise. When these implicit guarantees crystallize, governments often step in to keep the businesses afloat. In Azerbaijan, for example, the government intervened to bail out two SOEs, the International Bank of Azerbaijan and Azerbaijan Railways, which both required substantial support to meet debt obligations: $3.3 billion for International Bank of Azerbaijan and $600 million for Azerbaijan Railways, placing a significant fiscal burden on the budget. An IMF study determined that the average fiscal cost of SOE contingent liability realization globally was 3.0% of GDP, with a maximum of 15.1%.[28] This likely underestimates the true fiscal exposure that governments have to their SOEs. For example, corporate bond investors in SOEs often believed SOEs had implicit state support, influencing both pricing and availability of financing.[29]

---

[26]   ADB. 2020. *Guidance Note on State-Owned Enterprise Reform in Sovereign Projects and Programs.* Manila.
[27]   World Bank. 2021. *Debt Transparency in Developing Economies.* Washington, DC.
[28]   IMF. 2016. *The Fiscal Costs of Contingent Liabilities: A New Dataset.* IMF Working Paper. Washington, DC. The paper analyzed data from 80 countries, including 46 emerging market economies over the period 1990 to 2014, and identified eight instances of contingent liabilities crystallizing.
[29]   World Bank. 2017. *Financial Sector Assessment: Republic of Indonesia.* Washington, DC. p. 23.

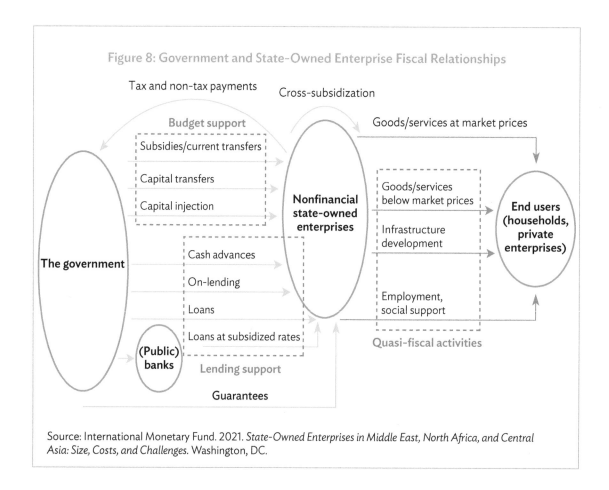

Figure 8: Government and State-Owned Enterprise Fiscal Relationships

Source: International Monetary Fund. 2021. *State-Owned Enterprises in Middle East, North Africa, and Central Asia: Size, Costs, and Challenges.* Washington, DC.

SOEs tend to not perform at the same level as equivalent private sector companies. ADB examined the return on equity and profitability of SOEs and concluded that, on average, SOEs lag private firms in profitability, which implies that SOEs have not been effective in earning a profit from the money governments as shareholders have invested. The analysis reveals that the rate of return for private companies exceeds that of public companies (Figure 9). ADB, in a study of returns, costs, and efficiency, concluded that measures of productivity and profit are less in SOEs than in comparator private companies (Figure 9). There are several reasons for the poor performance of SOEs. These include unfunded mandates that governments often impose considerable social objectives on their SOEs, without providing commensurate fiscal support, in the form of public service obligation payments. This means that SOEs cannot perform profitably, even if they were inclined to do so. SOE boards often lack the necessary independence from governments or the necessary capability and expertise to steer the operational and financial performance of the SOE. At the same time, oversight by government is often poor, with limited data provided or effectively analyzed. Poor financial and operational performance and weak corporate governance are reinforced both by perceptions and experience of government bailouts, creating soft budget constraints that are regularly breached. Where SOEs perform well, governments often see them as cash cows, draining them of their profitability and financial sustainability by imposing unreasonable dividend and tax policies on their well-performing SOEs. On occasion, governments become reliant on their strong-performing SOEs to prop up the government budget, making it difficult for SOEs to perform at this level over the long run.

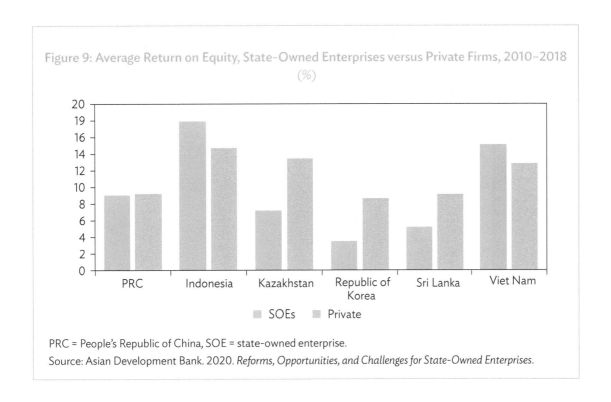

Figure 9: Average Return on Equity, State-Owned Enterprises versus Private Firms, 2010–2018
(%)

PRC = People's Republic of China, SOE = state-owned enterprise.
Source: Asian Development Bank. 2020. *Reforms, Opportunities, and Challenges for State-Owned Enterprises.*

When SOEs are not adequately and explicitly compensated for pursuit of socially important but noncommercial objectives, then an implicit subsidy is created, and government equity in such businesses is ultimately impaired. It is often suggested that comparisons with private firms are not useful since low profitability of SOEs is not usually seen as a major problem by policy makers. It keeps cost of service low, and the government does not want or need a return on its capital. This is not a sustainable fiscal position if the government does not provide a budgetary provision to cover the implicit subsidy. To illustrate this point, Figure 10 shows a hypothetical example where an SOE makes a net present value loss of 15 from an SOE investment project in which the government provided the equity financing. Due to the net present value loss, the full value of the investment will never be returned. Ultimately, if government delays recognition of this loss, it will overstate both the SOE's and government's financial position and will lead to a revaluation downward in the future. This creates an implicit subsidy and increases fiscal risk for governments, particularly if it results in a large fiscal shock when asset revaluations occur.

Implicit subsidies can be quite material in fiscal terms. In an analysis of SOE performance and levels of implicit subsidies during 2010–2018, for example, ADB found average levels equivalent to 2.5% of GDP in the People's Republic of China, 2.4% of GDP in Kazakhstan, and 0.6% in Indonesia (Figure 11). SOEs in Viet Nam, on the other hand, had an implicit surplus of 1.0% of GDP, suggesting the extraction of monopoly rents. Positive variations measured from the horizontal line suggest an implicit surplus and negative variation would represent an implicit subsidy.[30]

---

[30]   It is important to note that the fiscal impacts of ongoing implicit subsidies are real. The value of an asset on an SOE's balance sheet is defined by the cash flows it can create in the future. If equity and assets continue to diverge from revenues and profits, then a downward revaluation is inevitable.

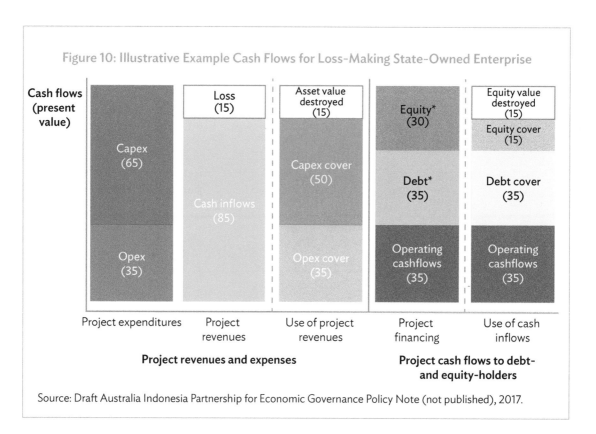

Figure 10: Illustrative Example Cash Flows for Loss-Making State-Owned Enterprise

Source: Draft Australia Indonesia Partnership for Economic Governance Policy Note (not published), 2017.

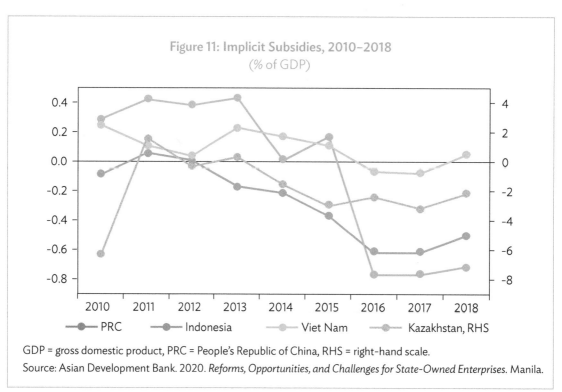

Figure 11: Implicit Subsidies, 2010–2018
(% of GDP)

GDP = gross domestic product, PRC = People's Republic of China, RHS = right-hand scale.
Source: Asian Development Bank. 2020. *Reforms, Opportunities, and Challenges for State-Owned Enterprises*. Manila.

If SOEs fail to return the equity invested in them, then their ability to leverage debt is limited. An important policy reason for establishing SOEs, rather than relying on government departments to deliver infrastructure services, is to ensure that infrastructure delivery is not constrained by the government's balance sheet, as SOEs can leverage based on their own performance. For example, a desired ("optimal") debt–equity ratio of 60:40 would allow each dollar of equity injected into an SOE to leverage an additional $1.50 of debt to be borrowed. However, if project cash inflows only cover 50% of project costs, the actual debt equity ratio will fall to 30:70. In such circumstances, rather than leveraging debt (and, hence, financing future investments), equity injections pay down existing debt.

An implicit subsidy arises if SOE project inflows do not return the equity invested in them, but the cost of that equity is never zero unless a government has zero debt. At a minimum, this suggests that equity investments in SOEs should generate a return of equity capital equivalent to the government's cost of borrowing. There is also a risk that in cases where governments seek to develop more private investment and competitiveness in sectors where SOEs operate with implicit subsidies, this can weaken the ability to attract private investment. This is not to suggest that governments should not subsidize certain goods and services delivered via SOEs, particularly where there exist positive externalities not being priced-in by the market. Governments appropriately deploy explicit subsidies in a range of forms, disclosed in their budget, including public service obligations, viability gap funding, direct provision of goods and services, and others. Implicit subsidies, on the other hand, have insidious fiscal impacts. They result in overstatement of government balance sheets with "investments" that do not provide a return and whose realizable value is very low or nonexistent.

A relatively low rate of crystallization of government contingent liabilities arising from the issuance of SOE guarantees does not necessarily indicate strong SOE health. A government's contingent liabilities through loan guarantees to SOEs could be estimated by assessing the probability that a guarantee would be called and the likely magnitude of the failure. Obviously, ongoing poor operational and financial performance may give rise to a guarantee being called. If, as discussed above, equity injections are functioning as implicit subsidies, they will, for a time, avoid a call on guarantees. Persistent poor financial performance that does not recover the cost of government equity will ultimately result in a downward revaluation, regardless of whether guarantees remain intact. Thus, the fiscal impact is the same, whether it manifests as a call on guarantee or a downward revaluation of government equity investment in SOEs.

SOE banks can provide an alternative for SOEs to borrow, without guarantees, placing fiscal risks and contingent cost of such borrowing on the balance sheet of the government, albeit indirectly. These arrangements have a very high contagion risk if, as is often the case, SOE banks are subject to directed lending and a high exposure to other SOEs and each other. In this case, a failing SOE could compromise the financial health of the banking sector. This results in SOE banks being overweight in the SOE sectors, and exposure limits and other prudential requirements may be weaker. Effectively, SOE banks would regard any SOE debt as being equivalent to sovereign debt. Even if there are no explicit sovereign guarantees, implicitly, SOEs and SOE banks are typically not allowed to fail. If an SOE that has substantial debt to one or more SOE banks is under financial stress and there is a risk of default, the government may be obliged to bail out both the SOE and the associated SOE banks. The SOE cannot be allowed to fail, as doing so would put the SOE banks under threat and create a risk of a collapse of the banking sector.

If properly managed and accounted for, guarantees are a valuable tool for attracting private investment, but are difficult to quantify and if they crystallize, have substantial detrimental fiscal effects. Some jurisdictions, such as Australia, charge guarantee fees calculated on the differential between the government's cost of debt at their credit rating and the SOE cost of debt at a notional lower "stand-alone" credit rating. This has two benefits: it makes transparent and explicit the cost and level of government support to the SOE and the real cost of service; and it ensures that infrastructure projects undertaken by the SOE are assessed against the real cost of debt rather than the subsidized on-lending or guaranteed cost of government debt.

Several governments are adapting reforms to increase commercial finance access by SOEs without government guarantees. These reforms aim to improve corporate governance, financial and operational performance, and reduce fiscal risks. According to the ADB publication, *The Bankable SOE: Commercial Financing for State-Owned Enterprises*,[31] an appropriate investment-grade credit rating is a prerequisite to improved access to commercial financing, and recognizes that to reduce country risk, governments should apply a consistent policy toward all their SOEs and incorporate full and transparent compensation. It also recognizes that good corporate governance is key to their ongoing financial and operational performance. These objectives are most effectively achieved if they form part of a broader reform effort focused on SOEs. The first step in the reform process is to consider whether SOEs are the appropriate delivery mechanism for a function or service. Governments should review periodically the status and viability of existing SOEs. According to the ADB publication, best-practice commercial policy frameworks would typically include the following:

(i)   The composition of the board of directors should foster board independence from management, sufficient to provide effective oversight. Board selection should rely on professional criteria based on an objective assessment of skills.

(ii)   Competitive neutrality between private companies and SOEs is important for economic efficiency. An SOE should not crowd out a competitive private firm based on SOE-specific procurement rules, tax policy, or regulation. Nor should arduous public policy mandates be allowed to competitively disadvantage an SOE.

(iii) Community service obligations mandated for SOEs should be compensated through transparent fiscal transfers from the public sector budgets to the SOE, with clear links to SOE performance and outputs to achieve the mandate.

(Iv)   SOE shareholders should be able to aspire for an "investment grade" rating. Such ratings can contribute to lower borrowing costs and tend to increase access to international capital markets.

(v)   SOE financial statements should meet the same auditing, accounting, and disclosure standards as listed companies in line with International Financial Reporting Standards.

The Ministry of Finance or equivalent plays an essential role in supervising the monitoring and reporting of SOE fiscal risks. Effective supervision is linked to periodic reporting on the fiscal impact of underperforming SOEs as well as provision of funds for fiscal risks. Public debt reports should also account for SOE debt that is guaranteed, but not provisioned in the state budget and non-guaranteed debt. This will help to ensure that government is informed on the size and impact of fiscal risks on the budget. It is entirely appropriate that governments subsidize goods and services delivered via

---

[31]   ADB. 2021. *The Bankable SOE: Commercial Financing for State-Owned Enterprises*. Manila.

SOEs, where there exist positive externalities not being priced-in by the market. But this must be done explicitly, to acknowledge and account in a timely and transparent manner for the quantum of subsidy that is being provided.

A ministry dedicated to overseeing SOEs or PPPs can help to reduce fiscal risks, but should also make sure it has the necessary institutional capacity to monitor and evaluate performance. Both modalities can realize efficiency improvements—but only if used as part of a robust and rigorous governance framework. This has been the case in advanced economies where there have been successful PPP programs delivering efficient infrastructure, and SOEs that are equal to or superior to their private sector peers. In Asia, the experience has been less positive. There are many SOEs that do not return their cost of capital and, thus, require implicit or explicit fiscal support from governments. Many PPPs have failed, been renegotiated, or otherwise did not meet expectations for service delivery. Nevertheless, there is substantial potential for greater efficiency in the delivery of public infrastructure through appropriate and effective use of these modalities. Unlocking this potential efficiency gain requires best practice project governance frameworks and a clear understanding of the appropriate use of SOEs and PPPs for infrastructure delivery.

Public–Private Partnerships as a Source of Fiscal and Debt Risk

PPPs, whether delivered through an SOE or a public sector ministry, are an opportunity to involve private sector efficiency, expertise, and capital in the provision of public infrastructure. Under the right circumstances, PPPs can provide VFM, despite the apparently higher cost of private debt and equity. PPPs can be a highly efficient infrastructure delivery mechanism. They have the potential to harness private sector incentives for performance and take advantage of the private sector's expertise and capacity for innovation. The ability of governments to price and manage risks, ex ante and through the entire project cycle, is thus crucial to achieving VFM from PPP arrangements. The failure to manage these risks effectively is, thus, a key source of PPP fiscal risk. If not properly managed, PPPs can reduce budget flexibility by the commitment public funds in long-term contracts, threaten the integrity of the budget process if treated off-budget, retard efforts toward fiscal discipline, and might well undermine macroeconomic stability in the event of a shock if adequate mitigation measures are not in place.

PPPs are prone to what the IMF describes as "fiscal illusion."[32] The illusion that PPPs fill funding gaps typically arises from a combination of factors, including accounting treatment, asset recognition criteria, and poor accountabilities for the management of contingent liabilities. By their nature, PPPs have characteristics that can obscure proper management and mitigation of fiscal costs and risk. Accounting treatment is a key source of fiscal illusion because cash accounting, common in many Asian countries, allows governments to increase infrastructure investment without creating an immediate and direct impact on public sector deficits or debt. While cash accounting provides this temporary benefit, over the project cycle the impact on government accounts is the same. For availability payment PPPs, the avoided up-front investment is offset by subsequent payments to the private partner covering the costs of construction, finance, and the operation of the asset. For user-pay PPPs, short-term budget savings during construction are equal, in net present value, to the user fees foregone during operation.

---

[32]   IMF. 2020. *Mastering the Risky Business of Public–Private Partnerships in Infrastructure.* Washington, DC.

Actual and Contingent Liabilities

PPP procurement is not always part of the formal budget process and is often characterized by no or weak central oversight. The nature of PPPs, whether provided through an SOE or a government ministry, can lead to perverse incentives for contracting agencies to procure infrastructure as a PPP over conventional procurement. This is because PPPs also frequently present opportunities (and incentives) for contracting agencies to disguise subsidies as contingent liabilities. Contracting agencies then do not have to accommodate the certain expenditure associated with the subsidy in their own budget, whereas contingent liabilities are managed centrally, if at all. An unrealistic patronage guarantee is a good example of this—if a specified traffic volume required to recover investment costs is almost certain not to be achieved, then it makes no sense that this not be recognized up front and accounted for transparently as a subsidy. However, many governments have put in place risk management guidelines, often with support from ADB and other donors, to improve how they manage actual and contingent liabilities (see Box, p. 23) making them less vulnerable to unanticipated fiscal consequence of PPPs.

Poor understanding of PPPs can cause actual and contingent liabilities to be poorly managed, disclosed, and hidden from scrutiny. The contingent liabilities—that is, payments contingent on certain future events occurring—are much less understood and usually their materiality, importance, and probability are glossed over by all government agencies and parties. Contingent liabilities are usually scattered throughout the web of interlocking contracts. Typical examples include:

(i)   **Exchange rate risk**. Many PPPs are wholly or substantially denominated in United States dollars or similar, creating obvious fiscal risk for the counterparty government.

(ii)   **Revenue guarantees.** It is common for PPPs where the demand for the service is variable (toll roads, urban transit, power purchase agreements) to have minimum patronage or usage levels.

(iii) **Compensation clauses.** For example, where the government commits to build complementary interface infrastructure, such as connecting roads or electricity transmission lines, and they are delayed. Compensation may also be payable if the government builds competing infrastructure.

(iv)   **Bankruptcy clauses.** If the private sector partner defaults, it is usual that the government guarantee repays the projects debt. In exchange, the government has the right to take over the asset.

(v)   **Termination clauses.** PPPs have numerous termination clauses for different circumstances. At a minimum, if the termination is triggered by the failure of the private party, the government must pay out the project debt in exchange for acquiring the assets of the project. At the other extreme, if the government terminates for no reason, it must pay out both debt and equity holders, including a sum for foregone profits.

Box: Fiscal Risk Management Reform in Armenia and the Philippines

Armenia: The Asian Development Bank (ADB), along with other development partners, provided technical assistance and programmatic support for the Government of Armenia to implement fiscal risk management reforms, improve transparency, and debt sustainability, and to include investment projects in the budget. Fiscal risk statements include on-budget lending to state-owned enterprises (SOEs) and other companies as reflected in the fiscal risk statements that accompany both the midyear medium-term expenditure updates and in the annual budget submissions. The fiscal risk management department at the Ministry of Finance (MOF) is preparing a comprehensive Fiscal Risks Statement for the Budget law. The statement presents a calculation of headline contingent liability exposures to major SOEs and selected public–private partnerships (PPPs), including power purchase agreements (PPAs) and a discussion on key fiscal risks.

The MOF is developing a more detailed and comprehensive stand-alone Report of PPP Contingent Liabilities as a "living-document" analysis application of the newly approved methodologies. It presents a more detailed calculation of contingent liability exposures per risk category regarding major SOEs and selected PPPs, and including PPAs. Going forward, the objective is to periodically update this reporting output and include its annual updates in the rolling Medium-Term Expenditure Framework with a disaggregation that fits within prospective sector ceilings. A PPP Contingent Liabilities Decree, including the requirements and related methodologies for identification of risks and reporting in documentation for the state budget, as well as obligations for benchmarking against PPP stock "fiscal affordability" ceilings, was prepared and submitted for interministerial review and approved by the Cabinet of Ministers of Armenia.

Philippines: ADB technical assistance supported the Government of the Philippines to improve development capacity constraints in the PPP program and address the accumulation of contingent liabilities. The government put in place risk management guidelines for contingent liabilities showing the commitment to providing funding to support the PPP program. The government launched a contingent liabilities fund to ensure capacity to meet direct and contingent PPP fiscal liabilities. The government created an interagency working group to monitor contingent liabilities of pipeline and ongoing PPP projects. The Bureau of the Treasury also established a methodology for valuing the contingent liabilities of PPP projects to create a better understanding of the impact of these risks.

These reforms have contributed to enhancing investor confidence, boosting the PPP pipeline, and increasing the resources available to support PPPs. The government considers PPP fiscal risks as part of its overall debt sustainability assessments. It includes PPP fiscal risks in the annual fiscal risk statements that offer a wide-ranging view of the overall country exposure to macroeconomic risks, contingent liabilities associated with the financial sector, SOEs, PPPs, local governments, and disasters.

Sources: ADB. 2022. *Regional: Improving Infrastructure and State-Owned Enterprise Governance for Sustainable Investment and Debt Management* (TA 6749); ADB. 2020. *Project Completion Report: Expanding Private Participation in Infrastructure Program in the Philippines*. Manila.

The ability of government ministries and SOEs to identify, price, and manage contingent liabilities, ex ante and throughout the project cycle, is arguably the single most important source of fiscal risk in PPP projects. Based on an analysis of 80 countries, including 46 emerging market economies over the period 1990 to 2014, the IMF quantified the average fiscal cost of PPP contingent liabilities as 1.2% of GDP (with a maximum of 2% of GDP).[33] It is worth noting that contingent liabilities need not be explicit to give rise to fiscal risks. Implicit contingent liabilities are not found in PPP contracts, but arise from the ultimate obligation to provide the service, typically due to public pressure from interest groups and consumers of the service among the public. This gives rise to the idea of the government as the risk bearer of last resort. Examples include sub-sovereign default by a private or public entity on non-guaranteed loans; other liabilities such as environmental damage, buyouts, bailouts; and central bank default on its obligations to allow repatriation of capital and profit.

Several DMCs deliver PPP arrangements through what are known as "institutional" PPPs, which are either completely publicly owned or under some form of joint venture arrangement with majority public ownership. In Indonesia, for example, SOEs are the dominant provider of toll roads under PPP arrangements. In the latter, Perusahaan Listrik Negara, the state-owned energy company, enters joint venture arrangements for most of its power purchase agreements, driven predominantly by a desire to share in the profitability of the business, while institutional PPPs provide an ability to assert some control over operations or at least over key decisions and to aid in transparency. Since risk transfer is a primary driver of VFM in PPPs, this objective can be undermined when risk, especially fiscal risk, is simply shifted from one part of the public sector (e.g., a government agency) to another (e.g., an SOE).

Many countries, however, have set up PPP units which typically identify projects as suitable for PPP procurement at the project selection stage, or earlier. Those selected projects then proceed through a parallel process without going through the budget and review process for traditional infrastructure projects. Although PPP units have many advantages in that they consolidate PPP expertise in one central place, the fiscal risk assessments by fiscal authorities at various stages of the procurement cycle would be important reforms to ensure that all projects, regardless of their ultimate implementation approach, pass through common project selection and appraisal processes.

Accounting Standards—Disclosure of Actual and Contingent Liabilities

Governance reforms focused on more effectively integrating PPPs with infrastructure planning, and the medium-term fiscal framework typically should include effective contingent liability management. Fiscal and contingent liability management should include a strong, standardized approval process with final approval by a central agency (usually the Ministry of Finance or Treasury), as well as setting limits and controlling usage appropriate to the fiscal circumstances. For actual liabilities, accounting International Public Sector Accounting Standard 32 (IPSAS) 32 recognizes that PPPs create assets and liabilities like those incurred under traditional procurement. The test for recognition of a PPP focuses on whether the government controls, through ownership, beneficial entitlement, or otherwise, any significant residual interest in the asset at the end of the contract. Adoption of IPSAS 32 generally

---

[33]   E. Bova et al. 2016. *The Fiscal Costs of Contingent Liabilities: A New Dataset.* IMF.

leads to the conclusion that most PPPs involve some degree of government control and, thus, should be recognized on the government's fiscal accounts. The World Bank and the IMF have developed a Public–Private Partnership Fiscal Risk Assessment Model (PFRAM) that allows governments to assess the fiscal costs and risks of PPPs through a structured process for gathering information by answering these questions: Who controls the asset? Who ultimately pays for the project? Does government give financial support for the private partner? How does the allocation of risk in the PPP contract risk affect the macro fiscal risks?[34]

Accounting standards also provide guidance for how contingent liabilities should be managed, disclosed, quantified and, if needed, provided for by direct budget allocations to provisions. IPSAS 19 says that if there is greater than a 50% probability that a guarantee will be called and the government can reasonably estimate the amount, the government should include a provision (liability) that is disclosed in the government's financial statements. Specifically, the standard specifies that the government should record an expense in the operating statement with the equivalent liability in the balance sheet. For current guarantees—disclosed previously as contingent liabilities—the government should recognize provisions in the accounting period in which the change in probability of a call occurs. This leads the way to providing for guarantees on a probability basis over time, building up a provision for the once-off payment through an annual expense allocation. Settlement payment of a guarantee claim is recorded against the liability. As part of managing contingent liabilities, many countries have imposed budget limits on annual PPP spending. This compensates for the lack of up-front recognition and partly as an implicit cap on contingent liabilities. Examples of such PPP spending limits include the Republic of Korea, which has a cap of 2% of government spending for PPP contracts;[35] Brazil, where PPP contract expenditures are capped at 3% of net current revenue for all levels of government; and Hungary, which caps the value of long-term PPP commitments at 3% of total state budget revenues in a budget year.[36]

---

[34] The PFRAM model is available at https://library.pppknowledgelab.org/both/documents/5782.
[35] *KDI Journal of Economic Policy.* Vol. 39 No. 1. 28 March 2017. pp. 41–82. https://doi.org/10.23895/kdijep.2017.39.1.41.
[36] K. Funke, T. Irwin, and I. Rial. 2013. *Budgeting and Reporting for Public Private Partnerships.* Washington, DC: IMF.

5. Governance Approach to Managing Fiscal Risks

Governance reforms to manage fiscal risks related to infrastructure investment rely on establishing fiscal targets and rules, national and sector planning, and the linkage to budgeting for public investment. Indonesia, for example, has a legislated deficit target of less than 3% of GDP and a debt–GDP target of about 30%. The Philippines developed a long-term vision and medium-term development plan, the 5-year Philippine Development Plan, which provides a comprehensive framework for the medium-term Public Investment Program and the Comprehensive and Integrated Infrastructure Program to implement the 5-year development plan. These reforms contribute to improved PIM. On the other hand, the PIMA analysis for Asia and the Pacific considers agencies responsible for project appraisal, project selection, maintenance funding, multiyear budgeting, and monitoring of public assets as the least effective PIM institutions in Asia.

The application of a Gateway assurance process can support project planning, preparation, and procurement to achieve better infrastructure provision and improve business planning. The role of the Gateway is to identify risks, including fiscal and climate risks, provide advice, and increase the potential for project delivery and benefit realization. A Gateway process should be linked to the PIM operational framework and the medium-term fiscal framework for major proposals that involve the investment of substantial government investment. The Gateway process plays a key role in the assurance approach designed to provide independent input into potential risks and mitigation strategies in major capital programs and projects, in alignment with government objectives and expected outcomes. In many countries, the cabinet tables and approves Gateway reports. This review is done at each major decision-making stage of the project cycle by another agency other than the procuring agency or by independent experts. Independent Gateway reports are then issued to procuring agencies to consider whether changes to business plans are required ahead of submission for final funding requests. The Gateway reviews cover the project cycle from initial needs analysis, the investment decision, and the procurement stage to decide if a PPP or traditional public procurement optimizes VFM, to project delivery and results. It should assess direct and contingent fiscal risk in the early phases of planning to ensure an investable and sustainable project is selected among the pipeline of potential projects.

Integrated Planning and the Budget Rule

Strong governance institutions are required for integrated planning to manage risks and avoid unexpected costs from infrastructure investment regardless of whether it is a PPP or delivered by an SOE or government ministry.[37] Best practice governance models are those in which the PIM operational framework is linked to medium-term fiscal framework processes. All projects should be derived from a

---

[37] For SOEs, this is relevant for publicly financed investment, including through direct budget allocation, government guaranteed borrowing, or through government mandates or assignments without an explicit funding source.

comprehensive medium-term infrastructure planning process based on strategic economic priorities. All public infrastructure projects, regardless of the mode of delivery, must be fully funded prior to obtaining financing and that governments select the best projects—those that deliver the most overall social and economic benefits to society. However, it is a challenge to implement a medium-term fiscal framework when governments come up against hard budget constraints that reduce the fiscal capacity to invest in needed infrastructure and services. For this reason, it is essential to select the most efficient and best projects to deliver infrastructure services. The selection of the best project is the "investment" decision, and is independent of, and comes before, the "procurement" decision, which determines how the project is best financed and delivered—through traditional type procurement or a PPP model—to maximize VFM.

The "budget rule" for infrastructure projects ensures that investment decisions are separate from procurement decisions. The government, usually through the Department of Finance or its Treasury, requires that the contracting agency justifies a proposed infrastructure project with a business case analysis based on a cost–benefit analysis. The government then examines the business case and decides if it can provide the required funding. The contracting agency incorporates the project budget into its forward capital and operating budget, to ensure that all proposed projects, regardless of procurement method, compete for the same funds which are by their nature finite sources of finance, thus, the need to ensure projects are prioritized based on highest net economic benefits and strategic importance. The choice of procurement method is not biased by the perceived budget impact, that is, the government does not maintain the common fallacy that modalities such as PPPs, SOEs, and special purpose vehicles are "off-balance sheet" with no debt or fiscal impact. After the project is fully funded, the procurement decision is based on analyzing which delivery modality delivers the most VFM. Government makes the procurement decision only after the project is worth investing in in the first place. Therefore, deciding to do a PPP or a traditional public investment project is a procurement decision, based on VFM considerations, and only after the government makes an investment decision. Once the procurement decision has been made, then the financial impacts must be incorporated into the forward budget, for example, the cost to the government for support through subsidies or contingent liabilities such as guarantees.

Subsidies Disguised as Guarantees

Contracting agencies may be incentivized to disguise subsidies as contingent liabilities, in the form of a guarantee, to avoid the immediate budget impact of the expenditure. This typically occurs when an agency seeking to proceed with an unviable project offers a minimum patronage and, thus, revenue guarantee. The project is approved based on plausible, but high patronage assumptions that suggest a low likelihood that the guarantee will be called. Once in operation, the situation changes rapidly, and the guarantee is triggered, and an effective subsidy paid. While a subsidy for the project may be justified, clearly the magnitude and impact have not been considered as part of the budget process. Given the considerable fiscal impact, a well-designed reform process for guarantees given to PPP proponents should:

(i)   **Place limits on the use and quantum of guarantees appropriate to the fiscal circumstances**. This will likely involve some quantification of the likely cost of guarantees through a probability weighted assessment or like set of limits.

(ii) **The benefits of a guarantee should outweigh the costs.** Control the circumstances in which guarantees are issued. Particularly for PPPs, the need for guarantees should be considered in the context of the overall risk allocation matrix between the private sector and the government and, thus, part of the VFM analysis. Partial guarantees should also be considered—that the guarantee covers only the first x percent of the loss. Central agencies should develop guidelines and rules to ensure whole-of-government consistency.

(iii) **Ensure a sound process of approvals.** Guarantees should go through a standardized approval process with final approval by a central agency and require a fully appraised business case.

(iv) **Charge guarantee fees**. This makes the real cost of service for SOEs explicit when they borrow using the government's balance sheet. For PPPs, some countries charge the line agency a guarantee fee to provide incentives to minimize use of guarantees.

Managing Contingent Liabilities

The management of contingent liabilities must start at the beginning of the project development process, even before it is decided to procure a project as a PPP or a traditional public investment. All public investment through the government or SOEs should be integrated within a country's PIM framework and be part of the normal capital budgeting process. In DMCs with substantial infrastructure gaps and relatively high pre-existing debt levels, it is tempting to see PPPs and SOEs as solving fiscal constraints. At best, this can delay the recognition of fiscal costs, but only temporarily. As such, a governance framework for contingent liability risk management should include the following stages:

(i)   **Disclose, value, and set limits on contingent liability stocks.** To understand the fiscal risk arising from contingent liabilities, the maximum potential exposure should be valued. The maximum exposure is best represented by payment under early termination for government default, quantified as project purchase of the outstanding debt and equity, plus compensation to the private provider. The stock of contingent liability changes over the project cycle; it is lowest at project award and end phases, increases during construction, peaks at commercial operation date, and declines during operational phases. The next step after disclosure of all contingent liabilities related to investments through PPPs or SOEs and valuation of the stock is to set some broad upper limits for overall contingent liability exposure.

(ii) **Estimate likely contingent liability flows.** Whereas contingent liability stocks value the maximum exposure, contingent liability flows are the annual expense payments expected from contingent liability crystallization. These flows are valued through probabilistic or scenario-based models to forecast contingent liability exposure, relying on the "stock" of contingent liability exposure, as estimated in Step 1. Probabilistic models take that stock—the value at termination—and applies a probability of failure. Failure rates can be modified by assessing project risk factors such as exposure to demand risk, payments in foreign currency payments, exposure to price setting by independent regulators, and unsolicited projects. Scenario-based models estimate a project's sensitivity to external factors such as macroeconomic shocks to forecast contingent liabilities. PFRAM can be used to estimate flows based on different scenarios, with the introduction of macro shocks into the model.

(iii)   **Create budget provisions for contingent liabilities.** There is no requirement for contingent liabilities that have not crystallized to be classified as liabilities in government financial statements. The IPSAS 19 requires that a non-crystallized contingent liability be classified as a liability if considered greater than 50% probable. More generally, it is prudent to keep a reserve of contingency funds, allocated annually from contingent liability flow estimates. Such reserves function as a financing mechanism where estimated lumpy future outflows are met through setting aside funds on an annual basis. The provisions may be funded or unfunded, depending on whether the government's financial statements are on a cash or accrual basis. Very few actively estimate likely contingent liability flows, and fewer still proactively provision for contingent liability risk as part of their medium-term budget processes.

6. Conclusions

One of the most important risks arising from poor performance by the SOE or PPP is the creation of fiscal risks and contingent liabilities—both implicit and explicit—through government loans, investments, and guarantees of investments. The Ministry of Finance or equivalent plays an essential role in supervising the monitoring and reporting of SOE and PPP fiscal risks through periodic reporting and disclosure of fiscal impacts, as well as provision of funds to manage contingent liability risks. Contingent liability governance will help attract high-quality investment, boost capacity to raise debt, and promote accountability. SOEs and PPPs tend to have complex, multidimensional fiscal relationships with government. Even in cases where there is no creation of a contingent liability and no government guarantee, government equity in an SOE or PPP project can be eroded if there is continuous poor performance and that requires additional government subsidies or investments that act as a subsidy.

Establishing a governance approach to managing fiscal and contingent liabilities of SOEs and PPPs revolves around three key components—establishing a Gateway assurance process, implementing integrated planning with a budget rule, and managing and disclosing fiscal and contingent liabilities.

(i) The Gateway process provides independent peer review at key stages of a project life cycle for major proposals that involve the investment of substantial government investment. A Gateway process contributes to improving planning and project preparation. It can identify risks, including fiscal and climate risks, provide advice, and increase the potential for project delivery and benefit realization.

(ii) Integrated planning requires that the PIM operational framework aligns to medium-term fiscal framework processes, and that projects derive from a comprehensive medium-term infrastructure planning process based on strategic economic priorities. The "budget rule" is a critical element of integrated planning in which all projects compete for available funds and are prioritized to invest in the projects with the highest economic and strategic benefits in line with country priorities. The procurement decision which chooses which modality—PPP or traditional investments—delivers the most VFM. After a decision is made to invest in a project, notwithstanding if it is a PPP, SOE project, or traditional public investment by a line ministry, the financial authorities need to manage fiscal risks and contingent liabilities.

(iii) Finance officials need to adapt a standardized process to disclose and manage fiscal risks and contingent liability stocks, set fiscal and contingent liability limits, estimate fiscal and contingent liability flows, and make budget provisions for fiscal and contingent liability risks. The management of contingent liabilities begins upstream in the project development process even before a ministry or SOE decides how to procure the project. All too often, projects suffer from optimism bias and the fiscal illusion where the probability of fiscal risks materializing is not adequately disclosed or accounted for in government financial statements.

Investment in public infrastructure should have positive effects on growth and the fiscal position, but this outcome is not guaranteed. The economic benefits will exceed the economic costs of an investment if it is in line with the Quality Infrastructure Principles for economic efficiency, social inclusion, disaster resilience, environmental and climate sustainability, and effective governance in infrastructure development. DMCs with stronger governance of the PIM (PIM) process are more likely to have predictable, credible, efficient, productive investments that deliver green, inclusive, and resilient infrastructure that meets economic objectives with greater development impact.

References

Asian Development Bank (ADB). 2020. *Asian Development Outlook. What Drives Innovation in Asia.* Manila.

ADB. 2020. *Project Completion Report: Expanding Private Participation in Infrastructure Program in the Philippines.* Manila.

ADB. 2020. *Reforms, Opportunities, and Challenges for State-Owned Enterprises.* Manila.

ADB. 2021. *The Bankable SOE: Commercial Financing for State-Owned Enterprises.* Manila. https://www.adb.org/publications/commercial-financing-state-owned-enterprises.

ADB. 2021. *Guidance Note on State-Owned Enterprise Reform in Sovereign Projects and Programs.* Manila. https://www.adb.org/publications/state-owned-enterprise-reform-sov-projects-guidance-note.

ADB. 2021. *Improving Infrastructure and State-Owned Enterprise Governance for Sustainable Investment and Debt Management.* Manila.

ADB. 2021. *Supporting Quality Infrastructure in Developing Asia.* Manila. https://www.adb.org/sites/default/files/publication/715581/supporting-quality-infrastructure-asia.pdf.

ADB. 2022. *An Infrastructure Governance Approach to PPP Value for Money Analysis.* Manila. https://www.adb.org/sites/default/files/publication/783341/value-money-public-private-partnerships.pdf.

ADB. 2022. *Asian Development Outlook 2022: Mobilizing Taxes for Development.* Manila. https://www.adb.org/publications/asian-development-outlook-2022.

ADB. 2022. *Regional : Improving Infrastructure and State-Owned Enterprise Governance for Sustainable Investment and Debt Management* (TA 6749).

Australia Indonesia Partnership for Economic Governance Policy Note (not published). 2017.

Bloomberg, M. et al. 2020. Emerging-Market Debt Crisis Brews as State Firms Need Rescue. https://www.bloomberg.com/news/articles/2020-06-11/rescuing-state-owned-firms-adds-to-emerging-market-debt-crisis. Cited in ADB. 2021. *The Bankable SOE.*

Bova, E. et al. 2016. *The Fiscal Costs of Contingent Liabilities: A New Dataset.* Washington, DC: IMF.

Ferrarini, B., M. Giugale, and J. Pradelli, eds. 2022. *The Sustainability of Asia's Debt, Problems, Policies, and Practices.* Manila: ADB.

Food and Agriculture Organization of the United Nations (FAO) Council, Hundred and Seventieth Session, 13–17 June 2022. Impact of the Ukraine–Russia conflict on global food security and related matters under the mandate of the FAO.

Funke, K., T. Irwin, and I. Rial, 2013. *Budgeting and Reporting for Public Private Partnerships*. Washington, DC: IMF.

Global Infrastructure Hub preliminary findings on quantifying the economic impact of infrastructure investment Third G20 Infrastructure Working Group: Virtual Meeting, 9 June 2020 Preliminary Findings.

Government of Japan, Ministry of Finance. 2019. *G20 Principles for Quality Infrastructure Investment*. https://www.mof.go.jp/english/international_policy/convention/g20/annex6_1.pdf.

Gupta, S. et al. 2014. Efficiency-Adjusted Public Capital and Growth. *World Development*. 57 (C): pp. 164–178.

International Monetary Fund (IMF). 2021. *State-Owned Enterprises in Middle East, North Africa, and Central Asia: Size, Costs, and Challenges*. Washington, DC.

IMF. 2020. *Mastering the Risky Business of Public–Private Partnerships in Infrastructure*. Washington, DC.

IMF. 2018. *Public Investment Management Review and Update*. https://www.imf.org/~/media/Files/Publications/PP/2018/pp042518public-investment-management-assessment.ashx.

IMF. 2015. *IMF Working Paper: The Macroeconomic Effects of Public Investment: Evidence from Advanced Economies*. https://infrastructuregovern.imf.org/content/dam/PIMA/Knowledge-Hub/Publications/pubdocuments/The%20Macroeconomic%20Effects%20of%20Public%20Investment%20Evidence%20from%20Advanced%20Economies.pdf.

IMF. 2015. *Making Public Investment More Efficient*. https://www.imf.org/external/np/pp/eng/2015/061115.pdf.

KDI Journal of Economic Policy. Vol. 39. No. 1. Public Private Partnerships and Fiscal Soundness of Local Government in Korea. 28 March 2017. pp. 41–82.

Kim, C. J. and Z. Ali. 2017. Efficient Management of State-Owned Enterprises: Challenges and Opportunities. *ADB Institute Policy Brief*. 4 December. https://www.adb.org/sites/default/files/publication/390251/adbi-pb2017-4.pdf.

Kose, M. A. et al. 2020. Caught by a Cresting Debt Wave. *International Monetary Fund*. 1 June. https://www.elibrary.imf.org/view/journals/022/0057/002/article-A012-en.xml.

New South Wales Treasury. 2017. *NSW Gateway Policy*. https://www.treasury.nsw.gov.au/sites/default/files/2022-04/tpp17-01_nsw-gateway-policy-expired.pdf.

World Bank. 2017. *PPP Reference Guide 3.0.* https://ppp.worldbank.org/public-private-partnership/sites/ppp.worldbank.org/files/documents/PPP%20Reference%20Guide%20Version%203.pdf.

World Bank. 2017. *Republic of Indonesia Financial Sector Assessment.* https://openknowledge.worldbank.org/bitstream/handle/10986/28391/Indonesia-FSAP-Update-FSA-07072017.pdf?sequence=1&isAllowed=y.

World Bank. 2020. *Benchmarking Infrastructure Development 2020: Assessing Regulatory Quality to Prepare, Procure, and Manage PPPs and Traditional Public Investment in Infrastructure Projects.* https://openknowledge.worldbank.org/handle/10986/34608.

World Bank. 2020. *Global Waves of Debt: Causes and Consequences.* Washington, DC.

World Bank. 2021. *Debt Transparency in Developing Economies.* https://documents1.worldbank.org/curated/en/743881635526394087/pdf/Debt-Transparency-in-Developing-Economies.pdf.

World Bank. 2022. *East Asia and the Pacific Economic Update: Braving the Storms.* https://openknowledge.worldbank.org/bitstream/handle/10986/37097/9781464818585.pdf.

World Bank. 2022. Food and Energy Price Shocks from Ukraine War Could Last for Years. 26 April. https://www.worldbank.org/en/news/press-release/2022/04/26/food-and-energy-price-shocks-from-ukraine-war.

World Bank. International Debt Statistics. https://databank.worldbank.org/source/international-debt-statistics (accessed 18 April 2022).

World Bank. PPP Fiscal Risk Assessment Model (PFRAM) Tool. https://library.pppknowledgelab.org/both/documents/5782.

World Bank, PPIAF. 2019. Who Sponsors Infrastructure Projects? Disentangling Public and Private Contributions. Cited in ADB. 2021. *Supporting Quality Infrastructure in Developing Member Countries of the Asian Development Bank.* Manilla.

Lightning Source UK Ltd.
Milton Keynes UK
UKHW050629170223
417164UK00031B/306

9 789292 697600